THE COMPLETE BOOK OF MAGIC TRICKS

Written by Jenny Lynch

Design: Julian Melhuish

Illustration: Michael Edwards

Editors: Nick Hoare & Simon Melhuish

Printed in Great Britain by Butler & Tanner Ltd, Frome.

Published by Lagoon Trading Company Ltd. PO Box 311, KT2 5QW.

CONTENTS

OFF THE CUFF - IMPROMPTU ILLUSIONS

IDIOT PROOF MAGIC

DANGEROUS MAGIC

MESSY MAGIC

DINNER PARTY MAGIC

PUB MAGIC

CLOSE-UP MAGIC

TRAVEL TRICKS

CHILDREN'S PARTY TRICKS

RISQUE MAGIC

INTRODUCTION

Who is he, so bereft of fancy, that cannot admit to a thrill of delight in seeing a Magical Act well performed? Who does not feel a shiver of excitement at seeing the seemingly impossible made real? Imagine how much greater the pleasure then, when one is the omnipotent, the perpetrator behind the Deed.

The Mysteries of the Magic Arts have fascinated and intrigued mankind throughout the ages. From the earliest days of pre-history, great men have striven to uncover the mysteries of the occult; some have ventured unto the very verges of the abyss, risking liaison with the Diabolical. How much easier is your task! A simple, diligent perusal of this volume will enable you to entertain and mystify your audience as assuredly as those past masters did.

The subtle secrets of all the famous classic conjuring tricks are explained within and all have been adapted for Home Performance. These are magic tricks with ordinary objects which can be practised within the domestic arena. The child at play, the husband in the tavern, the hostess at her dinner table: any one of these can now turn their hand to performing fantastic acts of magic.

This book spans a huge range of tricks; from hilarious pranks to truly astounding illusions. I have attempted to make your task easier by suggesting which tricks are most suitable for specific occasions. The categories will help you find your way through this book. If you are looking for illusions to perform at the dinner table for example, simply turn to the tricks listed under that category in the index.

The hour-glass icons relate the time required to learn to perform the tricks:

Tricks can be performed almost immediately.

Tricks require moderate practice.

Tricks will require some application, but are all the more impressive for that.

LEARNING THE MAGICIAN'S ART

Before proceeding, it is as well to stop here and remind ourselves of some of the basic principles of Magic. No matter how advanced or simple the trick you are about to perform, some laws remain immutable.

The chief of these is surely that, Practice Makes Perfect. You must never, ever perform a trick in front of an audience without first ensuring that you have had adequate practice. It is a good idea to practice in front of a mirror. This allows you to see your performance as your audience sees it and so allows you to detect any faults in your movements. It will also teach you where to position yourself in relation to your audience in those instances where the angle of observation is critical. Some of these tricks require a sleight of hand which will at first feel rather cumbersome, but with practice, the manoeuvre will become a mere reflexive action on your part and will be imperceptible to another's eye. Perhaps most importantly of all, practice will enable you to perform with absolute Confidence. You will be able to forget about the mechanics and instead concentrate on your most important task, that of entertaining your audience.

Never forget that you are first and foremost, an Entertainer!

A happy observer is a credulous one, so the more entertaining you are - the better it works for you. Your eager observers want to be amused and diverted and it is a good idea to guide them through each trick with a constant stream of witty discourse. It is worth taking the time to develop a "patter" which you feel comfortable with and which suits your personality. Your patter will also play a vital role in misleading the spectators at crucial points.

You will hear conjurors talk of the importance of Misdirection. This means diverting the gaze of your audience in the wrong direction. No matter how deft your hands become you will often need to achieve your aim covertly and so direct your spectators' eyes elsewhere. For instance, if you have an object hidden in your left palm it is imperative that you focus your attention elsewhere (possibly your right hand). You can tell the audience where to look either by means of your "patter" - when you challenge their gaze with your own - or by the physical disposition of your body.

OFF THE CUFF ~ IMPROMPTU ILLUSIONS

3

These "interludes" are very quick to perform but may necessitate a sleight of hand which will take some time to master. Once perfected, they can be performed anywhere, at any time, with the absolute minimum of preparation.

AN AMAZINGLY HASTY KNOT

(Required: a rope or twisted scarf)

This trick takes but a second to perform, and the more spontaneous it appears, the more dramatic and impressive the effect will be.

First, retire to the privacy of your bedchamber in order to practise the following manoeuvre. Hold one end of a piece of rope in the thumb crotch of your left hand. Drape the rest of the rope over the back of your right hand so that the end lies across your right palm.

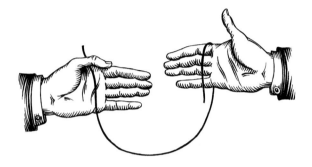

Bringing your hands together, take the left end of the rope up over the left hand with the first two fingers of your right hand. At the same time, clip the right end of the rope below the right hand with the first two fingers of the left hand.

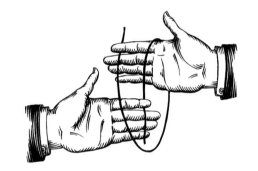

Now all you need do is pull your hands apart and a knot will miraculously form in the centre. Practise this until you can accomplish it very quickly.

To perform the trick, you could use a scarf or lady's silk handkerchief. Make sure that you show your audience that it is but a normal length of cloth with nothing "unusual" about it. Urge them to watch like hawks as your movements will be swift! If performed with awe-inspiring speed and accuracy, your audience will be left speechless!

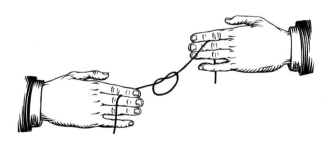

AS IF FROM NOWHERE!

(Required: one ball)

All master magicians know how to "palm" an object - that is how to hide it in their palm so that the audience have no idea that it is there. It is important that you are able to move your hand freely so that your audience suspect nothing. Here is how to do it!

Hold a ball in your fingertips. Then press it into your palm and close your thumb slightly so that the ball is, in effect, held in place and gripped by the muscle at the base of your thumb. Now take your fingers away so that the ball is held only in your palm. It should be held between the thumb and first finger, at the base of the thumb. If you keep your fingers curled slightly then this will not look stiff or unnatural. Practice with both

hands and with different sizes of ball.

To perform the trick, you need first to secretly palm a ball in your right hand. Start the illusion by facing left. Reveal your left hand, show it back and front, extending it to your left and bring your right hand up to point at your left hand. Swing your body round and face right and, at the same time, bring both of your hands together and "roll" the ball into your left hand. Remember to keep your fingers curled as this will conceal the transfer. Now bring your left hand up to point at the right hand and reveal that it is empty. Reach into the air with your left hand and Lo! - you can produce the ball at your fingertips.

A DICE ESCAPADE

(Required: a dice)

This is a very simple manipulation which needs to be presented with aplomb.

Close your left hand into a fist, keeping your thumb on the outside. Place the dice on top of your fist. Now move as if to take the dice in your right hand, but as your right hand goes over the dice, open your left fist slightly and let the dice fall into your left palm. All now depends on your powers of showmanship and misdirection.

You must direct the audience's attention to your right hand as if it contained the dice. Gaze at it intently and so will they.

Meanwhile keep your left hand relaxed. Use this opportunity to reach your left hand into your pocket for your magic wand and thus drop the dice in there. You can then tap your right fist before opening it to reveal that your hand is empty. The dice has disappeared!

Your friends will find this maddening to watch and will be completely mystified. The principle of misdirecting the audience's attention lies at the heart of most conjuring tricks. It is worth taking the time to master fully.

AN IMPRESSIVE
SINGLE-HANDED KNOT

(Required: a length of rope or ribbon)

First procure a length of silk ribbon or rope, whatever comes easiest to hand given your circumstances.

Hold your right hand out, with the palm towards your audience. Drape the rope over your right hand. The rope should be balanced so that there is a slightly longer length running over your palm (diag a). Move your little finger forwards so that the rope is clipped between your thumb and fourth finger (diag b).

Gradually start to turn your hand forward so that your thumb will point towards the floor. As you do this, bend your first and second fingers over and catch hold of the back part of the rope below your hand, and hold it between these two fingers. (diag c). Flick your hand so that the rope falls off the back. As you do so, change your finger grip so that your thumb and forefinger are holding the rope (diag d).

Practice this so it can be performed smoothly and quickly and the knot seems to appear as if by magic. Once you are confident, why not attempt a simultaneous knot in each hand?

(Diag a.)

(Diag b.)

(Diag c.)

(Diag d.)

AN UNPARALLELED KNOT

(Required: a length of rope)

This knot is a breathtaking feat to see performed and is guaranteed to raise a smile amongst even the most fractious of babes.

Hold the rope at each end between both hands. Bring the right end up behind the left and then over the wrist. You should now have a large loop hanging below the left wrist. Make sure that the loop is as large as possible.

Turn your right hand and bring it towards your body, passing the rope through the loop.

Now turn your right hand so that the fingers point towards the audience. At the same time, move the right hand up and forwards. What you now need to do is to let go of the right end of the rope and immediately grasp the rope at the point marked in the diagram, between your second finger and thumb. It will appear that you have simply shaken the rope from your wrists.

Although at no point did you let go of the ends of the rope, you have succeeded in tying a knot!

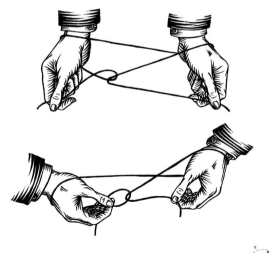

THE DOUBLE
CROSSING DICE TRICK

(Required: a dice)

This is a very simple yet very effective trick. It is perhaps most effective if you assume a naive persona and effect to be as surprised as your audience are.

Show your audience a dice, held between your finger and thumb, displaying one of its numbers. Turn your hand over and you show the opposite side and its number. Instruct your audience that it is one of the inherent properties of a dice, that the two numbers on opposite sides always add up to seven. But you can then baffle your audience by turning your hand and showing them that the original number has changed!

To do this, you must hold the dice as in the diagram.

As you turn your hand over to show the opposite face, make a quarter turn of the dice and the side pressed against your finger will come into view. Make a reverse quarter turn as you turn your hand back and the audience will actually never see the opposite side. Allow your audience to examine the dice and they will see that it possesses no extraordinary qualities - rather the magical properties reside in yourself!

A GIDDY DANCE

(Required: two balls)

You will leave your audience dizzy with this quick-fire interlude.

Place two large balls about 25 cm apart on the table. Say "one, two", as you place them down. Straight away, pick the left ball up with your left hand and the right ball with your right hand, again saying "one, two". Now put them down again, left then right, "one, two". Next put your hands down - palm upwards - on top of the balls, left then right, "one, two".

Now that you have established a rhythm, continue it!

Turn over your right hand, pick up the ball and apparently put it in your left hand, which closes as you say "one". Really you keep the ball in your right hand and your left hand moves away. Use your right hand to pick up the left ball as you say "two".

With both hands curled into fists, rap your knuckles on the table, saying "one, two". Then open your left fist and say "none", then your right fist, "two".

This trick takes but a little time to perform yet will dazzle your audience.

JUMPING JACK COIN

(Required: two coins)

This trick is simple to master and can be performed anywhere.

Reveal a coin in each hand. It is very important that the coins are positioned as shown. The left hand coin should be placed below the third and fourth fingers. The right hand coin should be near the base of the thumb. Hold the hands apart on a table top.

Now turn both hands over at exactly the same time so that the thumbs come close together and then draw the hands apart quickly.

Your audience will believe that there is a coin under each hand. Indeed that is a logical thing to think. In fact, because of the original positions of the coins, the right hand coin will have been thrown to the left and both coins will be under your left hand. All you need to do is practise to get the correct timing on this.

Lift the right hand to show that the coin has disappeared from there and then slowly reveal both coins under your left hand!

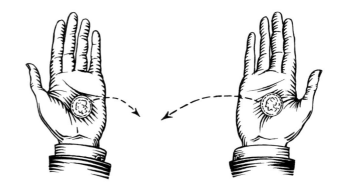

THE MELTING BALL SPOOF

(Required: a ball)

This is an utterly spontaneous illusion which can be practised anywhere.

Take a ball and hold it between the fingers and thumb of your left hand.

Bring your right hand towards your left and "appear" to take the ball; the thumb goes underneath and the fingers on top. As your right fingers close over the ball, let the ball actually drop into your left hand. You must then withdraw your right hand, to all intents and purposes as if it contained the ball. Drop your left hand casually to your side. The ball should be held loosely in the hand with your fingers slightly curled, holding it against the palm.

The success of this manoeuvre depends on you convincing your audience that the ball is in your right hand. In order to do this, you must "misdirect" all attention there. Make yourself believe that the ball is in your right hand and close your fingers as if they held the ball. Concentrate your gaze on your right hand and never, ever look at your left hand. Then, when you have built up this illusion, slowly "crumble" your fingers in a dissolving motion. Finally, open your fingers to reveal that the ball has "disappeared". Your audience will be dumbfounded!

This trick is very adaptable and can be performed with any small object which you find close to hand.

NOW YOU SEE ME!

(Required: a coin)

A classic, which no coin conjuror can afford to be without. First of all practice the following move.

Hold a coin in the palm of your right hand. As in the diagram, it should be placed at the base of your thumb.

Hold your left hand, palm up. Transfer the coin by turning your open right hand over the left. Withdraw your empty right hand and close the fingers of your left hand, covering the coin. Practice this in front of a mirror, making a precise mental note of the movements and timing involved.

Now do the same again, but this time, do not let go of the coin! This is best achieved by tightening the muscles at the base of the

thumb and fourth finger, just before you turn the right hand over. Thus the coin is retained in the right hand. Keep the fingers of this hand naturally curled slightly. You have just Palmed a coin!

The success of this action really depends on you misdirecting the audience's attention to your left hand. You should close the fingers of your left hand as if it contains the coin. All your concentration should be on that hand. Make yourself believe that the coin is there. Never, ever look at the right hand. Your audience will follow your gaze and expect the coin to be in your left hand. You should then open your fingers one by one, to show that the coin has in fact, vanished.

NOW YOU SEE ME!

(continued)

a.

b.

c.

d.

IDIOT PROOF MAGIC

Guaranteed to work every time, these "self-working" tricks are very, very difficult to get wrong! Some, for example, rely on the power of mathematics or the inherent properties of a dice. All are simple to execute yet appear to the uninitiated to be a veritable marvel of mystery.

A DEVILISH DICE PRANK

(Required: three dice)

Turn your back whilst one of your audience throws three dice.

Now, request that someone add up the numbers on the top faces of the dice and then lift up any one of the three and add to the previous sum, the number on the bottom face of that dice.

Beseech the volunteer to then roll this dice again and add to the last total the number of spots on its top face.

Turn to face the table. Remind your audience that you can not know which dice was thrown twice. Pick up the dice, concentrate very hard, and then boldly announce what the final sum was. All you need to do is, before picking up the dice, add 7 to the spots showing on the top faces of the dice.

The sum of the dots on all pairs of opposite faces on a dice is 7 and it is this feature which lies at the heart of the trick. The final sum to be guessed is the number of points on the upper faces of the three dice in their final position plus the sum on two opposite faces of a dice (which is always 7). However, presented with wit, this simple trick can appear utterly baffling to observers. You must take care not to make it appear too easy; stare wildly at a distant fixed point, pace the room and generally behave as if striving for illumination.

FOUR SCURVY KNAVES

(Required: a pack of playing cards)

This card trick is very simple and requires no complicated sleight of hand. Rather its success depends on your storytelling ability - feel free to elaborate on the narrative and all listeners, young and old, will be thrilled!

Present a pack of cards to one of the assembled and ask them to remove the four knaves from the pack. Explain that the pack represents a grand old house and the four knaves are wicked and treacherous thieves intent on purloining the riches from the house.

The thieves work as a team, each with their own task so that they can operate as quickly and as efficiently as possible.

The first thief goes to ransack the basement (place one knave to the bottom of the pack).

The second knave goes up to the roof to search the attic (place one card to the top).

Now cut the pack, looking all the while at the two remaining thieves. It is good if you can arrange it so that these two remaining are of the same colour. You should break off here and go on a seeming diversion: explain that the remaining two knaves are brothers (hence the colours). They are in fact cowardly burglars who are unnaturally dependent on each other. They remain outside the house arguing furiously as they are reluctant either to be parted or to go to either extreme of the house. Describe their quaking terror and staring eyes until your audience are in peals of laughter.

A compromise is finally reached and the brothers decide to go together to the centre of the house. Distract your audience so that - as you place the two knaves on top of one of the piles and then place the other pile on top of them - they will indeed believe that you have consigned them to the middle of the house. What you have actually done is to place them on what was the upper packet of the deck, and placed what was the lower packet on top of them. Thus you have brought all the thieves together in the middle of the house.

Explain that the arguing of the two brothers alerted a neighbour who called the police. Describe the rush of the police to the house and the horror of the thieves as they fall over themselves, scampering in their confusion to the centre of the house.

VOILA!- there they are, ready to be apprehended by the Superintendent! Fan the pack to reveal the four knaves gathered together in the middle.

A MIRACULOUS DIVINATION

(Required: three dice, pencil and paper)

Turn your back and ask a volunteer to roll the three dice and arrange them in a row so that their top faces make a three digit number.

Ask them to add to this the three digit number given on the bottom faces of the dice. The resulting six digit number they need to divide by 111 and tell you the result. From this, you can tell them what is on the top faces of the dice.

To do this, you merely need to subtract 7 and then divide by 9.

In our example, the top faces give	254
Number from bottom faces	(523)
254523	
Divide by 111	2293
You subtract 7	2286
You divide by 9	254

The secret is completely undetectable - and it always works!

NUMBER CONUNDRUM

(Required: pencil and paper)

This trick revolves round the magical properties of the number three. Your volunteer needs to be able to multiply by three, or indeed, a pocket adding machine can be used.

Request that a volunteer thinks of any two digit number and writes it down. Meanwhile, inform your audience as to the magic properties of the number three and draw a large triangle on a piece of paper.

Ask your volunteer to MULTIPLY his number by 3.

Now he should ADD NINE (which, being three multiplied by three is especially magical)

Now MULTIPLY the result by 3 again.

Finally, entreat him to ADD THE ORIGINAL NUMBER.

This total should be written in the centre of the triangle.

The total will be a three digit number. Circle the last two digits and concentrate furiously on the number. You need no further information now, before you announce the original chosen number.

In fact you ignore the last digit altogether. The encircling is a deliberate misleading act on your part. All you need is the first two digits from which you subtract two.

For example: $52 \times 3 = 156$

$$156 + 9 = 165$$
$$165 \times 3 = 495$$
$$495 + 52 = 547$$

so the answer is $54 - 2 = 52$.

If your volunteer originally chose 99 or 98 then the result will be a four digit number. In this instance, you should subtract two from the first three digits.

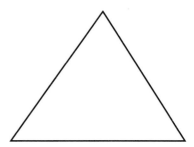

THE REMARKABLE
CARD REVELATION

(Required: a pack of playing cards)

This trick takes no time to learn but is nonetheless impressive for all its simplicity.

First of all, shuffle and fan out a deck of cards, keeping them face down.

Ask one of the company to pick a card from the fanned-out deck and show it to the assembled company. This guarantees that the value of the card will be remembered, but, more importantly, it also creates a diversion during which you gather the remaining cards up and notice which card is on the bottom of the pack. Remember this card. It is what is known as your "Key Card".

Cut the pack at random and place the two piles on the table. Take the chosen card and replace it, seemingly at random, onto one of the piles. In reality, make sure that it is the pile which was uppermost when the pack was complete. Now place the other pack on top of this one, so that it seems that the chosen card is now lost amidst the others.

Deal the cards out from the top of the deck, turning them over as you do so. Build up an expectant atmosphere, telling your audience that you feel you are drawing near. As you turn over what was the bottom card, exclaim excitedly that you believe the next card to be the one! And so, of course, it is!

THE RING THAT PASSED
THROUGH A ROPE

(Required: two rings, a piece of rope)

This trick is impossible to get wrong and takes but a minute to perform. It is one that you can safely repeat several times and your audience will still be none the wiser!

Firstly, thread the rope through both rings. Inform your audience that there are two ways to take the rings off the rope. Method one is to take the ring off the end of the rope.

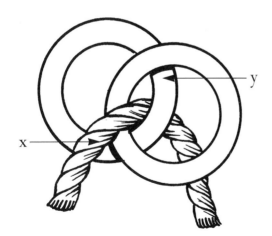

The "magic method" is to keep hold of the ends and take the ring through the rope and off the middle.

You can achieve this thus: use your left thumb and finger to hold the rope and ring firmly at point x and your right thumb to grasp the ring only at point y.

Pull your right hand quickly down and slightly back towards you and off the end of the rope. You have taken the ring in your right hand off the end of the rope but will also find that the ring held in your left hand is no longer on the centre of the rope either.

The ring has passed through the rope at stupefying speed!

STAR STRUCK

(Required: two dice, pencil and paper)

For this you will need a five-sided star drawn on a piece of card plus two dice. Beseech your audience to throw a dice whilst your back is turned and to cover it with a piece of paper or handkerchief. You will now endeavour to find out the value thrown.

A suggested patter might run as follows:

"Kindly observe the two horns on the star. In the Devilish art of Black Magic these horns always point upwards. Here you will observe that the horns point downwards as we are dealing with White Magic. These horns are of the utmost importance so would you kindly MULTIPLY BY TWO the number you have just thrown?"

"Now you will observe that the star has five sides. Would you kindly do me the honour of ADDING FIVE to your last number"

"In fact, five is a very significant number as the star also has five points. Could you please MULTIPLY your last number by FIVE?"

"Finally, could you throw a second dice, whilst my back is turned and add the number thrown to your last number? Now write the total in the centre of the star and please ensure that both dice are covered when I turn to face the table."

All you now need to do is subtract 25 from the total. The resulting two digit number will represent the two numbers on the dice eg. 68 - 25 = 43. So the first dice is a four and the second, a three.

THE THREE FAN CARD TRICK

(Required: a pack of playing cards)

Some card tricks can be very complex. This one is relatively simple and so is a good place to start. The wonderful thing is that it is self-working: as long as you can remember how to spell Abracadabra, success will always be yours!

Deal three piles of seven cards each, face down. You can discard the rest of the pack. Ask a spectator to pick one of the piles. Display the cards in the chosen pile in a fan, facing the audience. Ask your volunteer to pick a card but not to tell you what it is.

Place this pile between the other two piles. Deal the 21 cards one at a time, again into three piles. Pick up each pile one at a time and display it to the spectator, asking them to identify the pile which contains the chosen card. Once again, place this pile between the other two and deal out the cards one at a time into three piles. Fan out the cards for the third time and ask the spectator to identify the pile containing the chosen card and place this between the other two piles.

Now is the time to introduce the magic incantation "ABRACADABRA". Urge stillness and concentration from your audience. Instill in them, some sense of the gravity of the powers to be invoked. Spell the word out, in a reverent tone, placing one card on the table for each letter spelled. The very next will indeed be the CHOSEN card!

A TOWER OF GENIUS!

(Required: three dice)

Ask a volunteer to arrange the dice in a tower, as shown. Make sure that they are happy with their arrangement and allow them to change it if they wish. Explain to your audience that there are five faces which are hidden from view: those on the four faces where two dice touch each other and the face on the bottom of the tower. Your magical powers are such that you can see what these hidden faces are, without disturbing the dice tower.

How? In the diagram shown, the answer is 16. The fact that the opposite faces of a dice always add up to seven, lies at the heart of this trick. thus, the top and bottom of the middle dice add up to 7, the top and bottom of the bottom dice add up to 7 more. The bottom of the top dice is 2 (7 minus the top of the dice). This is a simple trick but it can be presented to devastating effect. You should call for absolute silence from your audience as you concentrate very hard on the tower; imagine that you are indeed looking through the dice to the hidden faces!

THE UNCANNY
POWER OF NUMBER 1089

(Required: a balloon, pencil and paper)

This is an ingenious and cunning trick which will convince your audience that you have the power to foretell events. A calculating machine may be needed.

Write down the number 1089 on a piece of paper and slip this inside a balloon. Blow the balloon up and tie it so that the paper is secure inside.

Turning to your audience, ask a volunteer to think of any three digit number in which the first and last digits differ by a minimum of 2. Let us suppose 643 is chosen.

Ask them then to reverse that number and subtract it from the original number: thus 643 - 346 = 297.

Finally request that they reverse the answer and add it on: 297 + 792 = 1089. Ask them what their final number is.

Now turn back to the balloon and request that one of your audience burst it, using a pin. The piece of paper will be revealed and on it, the answer, 1089. In every instance, as long as the first and last digit differ by at least 2, the answer will always be 1089.

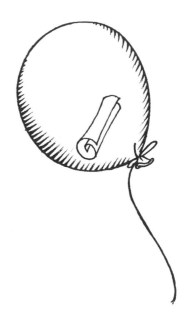

A CURIOUS SHUFFLE

(Required: a pack of playing cards)

You need only ten cards for this illusion and you must secretly pre-arrange the order. They will appear to be in a totally random order but should however, be arranged thus:

8, 3, 5, A, 9, 10, 4, 6, 7, 2

starting from the top, with the cards face downwards. They may all be of one suit if preferred. False shuffle these so that the order is unchanged. (See "CONFOUNDING COLOURS" for details of the False Shuffle).

This will convince your audience that the cards are in no special order. Announce that you are about to perform a "Magic Shuffle".

Put the first card on the table, the next card under the remaining eight cards you are holding, the third on the table, the fourth under the remaining cards you are holding and

so on until all the cards are on the table. Now look at the cards. Oh Dear! Affect great consternation and dismay! The Magic Shuffle did not work on this occasion because you forgot the magic incantation. Reveal the cards to be still hopelessly muddled.

Appeal to one of the assembled to see if they can make it work by using the magic word. Hand them the packet and beg them to execute the Magic Shuffle just as you did but this time uttering the Magic Word. It can be any word you choose, Allabazooka, Witchidykooka, Fliperdeedodah....

Once they have performed the Magic Shuffle, let them deal the cards face upwards in a row. They will be in perfect order from one through to ten!

DANGEROUS MAGIC

Illusions for the confident conjuror, these require real nerve and daring and need to be presented with aplomb. Some require that a spectator risk a limb, others involve objects boring their way through furniture or flesh: either way, they are not for the faint hearted.

THE CRUMBLING TUMBLER

(Required: a coin, a glass and a sheet of newspaper)

You need to be actually seated at a table for this to work. Your powers of Misdirection will be tested to the full!

Place the coin on the table in front of you and announce that you will make it pass through the table. Place the glass over the coin. Explain that the coin is actually very shy and surely will not make its journey in full view of the audience. Wrap the newspaper very firmly around the glass so that its outline is still quite visible.

Make some hand movements over the glass and utter an incantation. Remove the glass, still holding it through the newspaper and - oh! Affect great consternation as you observe that the coin is still there!

Cover the coin once more and repeat the above. This time as you remove the glass, bring it to the rear edge of the table. As you

lean forward to look at the coin, which is still very evidently "there", drop the glass from the newspaper onto your lap.

The paper will still hold the shape of the glass so no-one will realise that the glass is no longer there. You must make sure you handle the paper as if it still contained the weight of the glass. Try the trick again, simulating great dismay all the while. Finally announce that you believe it would be easier to pass the glass through the table. Crush the paper down onto the table top. Your audience will squeal with dismay and may even rush to your aid expecting you to be covered in shards of glass. All you have to do is calmly reach under the table and remove the glass from your lap. Bring it out as if you had really made it pass through the table!

THE KING OF ROPE ILLUSIONS

(Required: 20 / 30 / 60 cm lengths of rope)

This is a truly impressive illusion for the confident conjuror. Though the following moves appear quite tricky, if you go through them slowly at first, with the ropes in your hand as you do so, you should not encounter much difficulty. Show your audience each length of rope and place them like so: the longest piece into the thumb crotch of your left hand, the medium piece alongside it, beside your finger and thumb, and finally place the shortest piece alongside that.

Firstly, you need to bring all the lower ends of the ropes into your hand like so:

Using your right hand, bring the lower end of the long piece and place it between the top ends of the medium and short pieces. (diag b)

Then lift the lower end of the medium piece and place it to the right of the top end of the short piece. (diag c)

Now place your right hand through the loop formed by the long piece, take the lower end of the short piece and place it to the right of its other end. (diag d)

Take the three rope ends on the right in your right hand and pull them to the right, keeping the other three rope ends firmly held in your left hand. It will now look as if all the ropes are of the same length because the short and long length are looped together and this loop is concealed in your right hand! (diag e & f). This will provoke gasps of delight from your audience.

You will now count each rope individually from hand to hand to show that the ropes are of equal length.

To do this you will perform what is known as a "false count". Take the medium rope from your left hand, with your right, and count "one". Moving your right hand back to your left, replace the medium rope into the thumb crotch and use your second and third fingers to grasp the short and long ropes and move them to the right, "two". As you count "three" move the medium rope again from the left hand. It will appear that you have counted the ropes singly and that they are all of the same length!

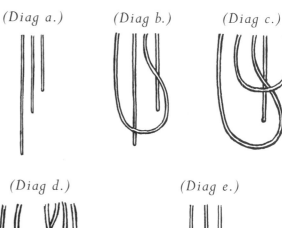

(Diag a.) *(Diag b.)* *(Diag c.)*

(Diag d.) *(Diag e.)*

THE KING OF ROPE ILLUSIONS

(continued)

As the last rope is counted, throw it over your shoulder and apparently tie the other two pieces together. (You should have the medium length over your shoulder and the long and short in your hand). All you do is tie the short piece across the centre of the long piece. It will look like two pieces of equal length tied together. (diag g)

Take the piece thrown across your shoulder and tie it to the end of the long piece. The audience will believe that you are showing them three equal pieces if rope held together by two knots. (diag h)

Now wind the rope around your left hand. Make sure that the genuine knot (ie. the last one which you tied) goes into the palm of your left hand. The other knot is only a slip knot (the short piece tied around the long piece). Slide this down the rope and keep the short piece in your right hand as you continue winding the rope. Draw your audience's attention to the rope around your left fist as you hide the false knot in a pocket or somewhere else convenient.

Slowly unwind the rope from your hand until you reach the knot. Take the knot in your right hand, thus concealing it, and continue unwinding the rope. It now looks as if all three ropes have been miraculously made into one. All that is left is for you to graciously accept the applause.

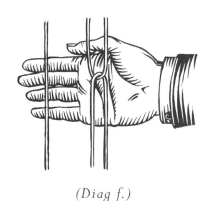

(Diag f.)

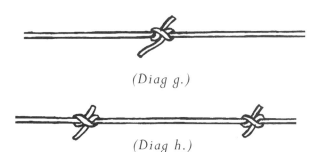

(Diag g.)

(Diag h.)

A STUNNING PULL THROUGH

(Required: scarf or large twisted handkerchief)

Beseech one of the assembled to proffer their arm for your use. Satisfy them that no harm will come to the limb.

Place the scarf on top of their arm, gather the ends underneath and pretend to tie a knot. In reality, you simply gather the centre of each side of the rope or scarf, make two loops and fold them together.

Pull the loops tight and then bring the two ends together above the arm and tie as many knots in it as you can. It will appear that the rope is securely tied around your volunteer's arm.

Grasp the knotted ends. Heighten the audience's excitement by reminding your volunteer of the infinite amount of bodily stillness required. Urge your audience to concentrate hard and once a tense silence has descended, suddenly pull the rope upwards. The rope appears to travel straight through the arm, much to the unbounded astonishment of all onlookers.

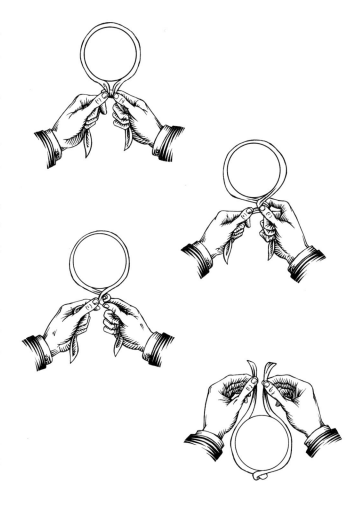

A WONDROUS TEST OF NERVE

(Required: two empty jam jars and a banknote)

There is nothing "mysterious" about this trick but the audience participation which it encourages is an invaluable part of any magic act.

You need first to procure a bank note from one of the assembled. Assure your friend that the note will be returned in one piece! Next you must balance the jam jars on top of each other - the top one being upside down so they are "neck to neck". In between the two place the bank note. The challenge is to remove the money without moving or touching the jars.

Your spectators will be full of nervous dread as they visualise possible disaster. Once people have had a go - or shied away as the case may be - you can boldly show them the solution.

Hold one end of the banknote and pull it taut. With the index finger of your other hand strike down sharply on the note about half way between your hand and the jars. The note will come free and the jars remain in position.

You should practice this movement until you are fully confident with it and can perform it with impressive flamboyance!

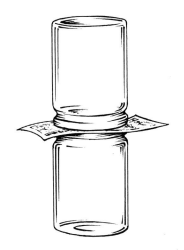

MONEY GO ROUND

(Required: six coins, blu-tack)

This trick needs to be performed at a table which does not have any sort of table cloth. You will need six coins.

Show the assembled four coins which you place on the table, not far from where you are sitting. Now entreat one of your audience to assist you. Ask them to attach a small piece of Blu-tack or Plasticine to another coin and to stick that coin on the underside of the table, approximately eighteen inches away from you.

Show that both your hands are empty and sweep the four coins with your right hand into your left. Close your left hand immediately and place it above the coin hidden under the table.

"Dear friends," you observe, "as soon as that coin under the table knows that there are more coins above it, it will endeavour to bore its way through to join its friends. If you concentrate very hard, you may be able to hear it." You should lower your head, turning one ear towards the spot. Finally you are able to open your hand and reveal five coins there. Invite your audience to look under the table and they will see that the coin has gone.

The effect is achieved thus: a duplicate coin is pre-set, attached to the underside of the table very close to where you are sitting. As your volunteer sticks a coin under the table, you can casually rest your hand on the edge thus screening the coin already there.

After you have shown that your hands are empty, place your left hand just under the table, to receive the coins as they are swept into it by your right hand. As you take your left hand away, your fingers need to detach the duplicate coin. You must close this hand before you raise it and place it on the table.

The five coins are now already in place and you merely need to lose the coin stuck under the table by your volunteer. As you lower your head to listen, you will inevitably lean forward. This gives you ample opportunity to detach the coin with your right hand. You can either hide it in your sock or shoe or even down your cuff. Unobtrusively, let it be seen that your right hand is empty.

You can enhance the effect of this trick by making scratching noises with your finger as the coin "bores" it way upwards through the table.

THE PHENOMENAL
TRANSMOGRIFYING COIN

(Required: a coin)

In this illusion you will appear to pass a coin right through your fist. You will need unflinching nerve and audacity to perform this as it is greatly improved by some devious acting on your part.

Reveal your left hand to the audience so that they can see that it is empty. Then close it into a fist and hold it out with the back of your hand uppermost. Now reveal the coin, held between the fingers and thumb of your right hand and press it firmly against the back of your left hand. Move your right hand back and forth as if you really were trying to press the coin through your hand.

Now remove your right hand, with the coin hidden from view, as if you had actually succeeded. Open your left hand confidently and then feign great dismay when you see that the coin is not there. "What is this? Maybe I did not push hard enough. One final attempt....."

Now, close your left hand and turn it over at the same time as you bring your right fingers onto the back again. It is as if you are about to repeat the trick. What the audience do not see however is the coin dropped from your right hand into your left just before you begin to close the left. Blatant misdirection is called for here. Be sure to engage your audience as you perform this move, castigating yourself that you have to try a second time. If you look at your audience as you do this, they will be looking at your face and not at your hands.

Once again, rub the back of your left hand until you are satisfied that "the coin has passed through the flesh". Reveal the coin in your left palm and show your right hand to be empty. A true fusion of mental and physical adroitness is called for here in order to deceive and mystify your spectators.

MESSY MAGIC

The entertainment to be had here revolves round challenging your audience to participate! Spectators should be prepared to run the risk of a thorough dousing.

HOW THE PENDULUM SWINGS

(Required: a cup of water, some string, scissors)

Tie a piece of string around the handle of a cup which is half filled with water. The cup must not be too full; you need to be able to lift it into the air by the string without spilling any of the contents. Hand the end of the string to a spectator and challenge them to cut the string with a pair of scissors but not let the cup fall. They cannot rest the cup on any other object or hold the string beyond the point at which they cut it. Watch them puzzle over this. It seems impossible until you know how!

Show your good friends by taking the string and winding it slowly around your finger. Take some of the string up, make a loop and tie it in a knot. Now all you have to do is cut the rope through the loop. The knot keeps everything in place and the cup remains safe - though it may be swinging perilously!

AN ICED DELIGHT

(Required: two glasses of water, some ice and some string)

More of a brain-teaser than a magic trick this will nonetheless, provoke much hilarity amongst your party.

All you need are two glasses filled with water, each with a single ice-cube floating in it. One of these you give to your onlookers, along with a length of string.

Challenge your fellows to remove the ice-cube from the glass, using the length of string. They are not allowed to touch the ice with any part of their body! Stand well back as they get very damp, attempting to "lasso" the ice cube with the rope. Spirits will be high and indeed, some lucky fellow may actually accomplish this. There is however a much easier way and it is far more likely that they

will turn to you with weary hearts and declare, "this is impossible!"

What you must do while they are preoccupied is, lay your loop of string on top of the cube so that it lies flat, and secretly sprinkle some salt across both the string and ice cube. In a very short time the string and ice will have fused together and you will be able to lift the cube clear of the glass.

A SPLIT BANANA

(Required: a banana and a needle)

Some advance preparation is called for here. Take a banana and insert a needle through the skin, picking a dark part of the fruit so that it will not leave a tell-tale mark. Gently twist the banana so that the needle is, in effect, slicing it inside its skin. Repeat this at regular intervals down the length of the fruit - say three or four times.

Now give the magic banana to one of your unsuspecting observers and request that they peel and eat it. How surprised they will be, to discover that you have succeeded in slicing it for them!

PHANTOM FROM THE FARMYARD

(Required: an egg, some glitter, paper and paste)

This requires some delicate preparation but is well worth the effort. Make two small holes with a sharp needle, one at each end of an egg. Now blow through one of the holes to remove the contents. Very carefully, wash the shell and leave it to dry out.

Next, carefully cut a hole in the side of the shell, about the size of your finger-tip. Fill the shell through this hole with glitter. Cover the hole with some paste and a piece of paper the same colour as the egg shell.

You may now select your victim - hold the egg either over your own head or somebody else's! Either way, build up suspense. Hold the egg up high and crush it, grinding your thumb forcefully into the shell. Your audience will be amazed to see a shower of glitter rather than the expected sticky mess.

A SPECTACULAR BALANCING ACT

(Required: a toothpick and a glass of water)

This trick is best performed towards the end of dinner, when the tablecloth is somewhat rumpled and disarrayed.

You need to be able to conceal a matchstick or toothpick under the cloth so that it cannot be seen. Obviously you need to choose the right moment at which to do this - pick a moment when the others are deep in conversation and you are unobserved.

Next, procure a glass which is about one quarter full of water (or some other liquid refreshment) and declare that you are about to perform a miraculous balancing feat. Tilt the glass at an angle and attempt to steady it there. Use both hands as the glass will surely wobble alarmingly. Until, that is, you succeed in locating the matchstick! Then remove your hands to reveal the glass perfectly poised.

You will need to practise this as, in truth, it is not as easy as it sounds - even with the help of the matchstick. Make sure that the concealed matchstick is near your body and so will not be spotted by your audience. Practice to determine what the optimum amount of water is. Build up suspense. Show how difficult the balancing is and, once you have succeeded, be ready to catch the glass swiftly, as if it were about to fall at any moment.

There is unlimited fun to be had as you pass the glass on and challenge your friends to try their hand. They can practice until Doomsday with nothing but a damp table cloth to show for their efforts!

THE TREMBLING THIMBLE

(Required: four egg cups, four larger beakers, a thimble and thread)

The cups need to completely cover the egg cups when they are placed over them. Fill one of the egg cups with water and request one of the assembled to arrange the egg cups in any order - whilst your back is turned. Before you turn round, they must cover each with one of the larger cups.

Now show the audience your magical "water diviner". This is a thimble with a long piece of string tied round the top of it so that you can swing it like a pendulum.

Explain how "like attracts like" and fill the thimble with water. Now hold the thimble over each cup in turn. At one of the cups the thimble will begin to swing alarmingly. When the cup is removed, this is revealed to cover the egg cup filled with water.

You achieve this trick thus: The egg-cup filled with water has a human hair stuck to its underside. This should be just long enough to protrude beyond the covering cup. This will be invisible to the audience but should be enough to guide you. Be careful not to let anyone see you looking for the hair - you must concentrate hard on the thimble by way of "misdirection".

You can make the thimble move yourself by adjusting your fingers only ever so slightly. Once again, it all lies in the acting: effect surprise and your observers will share in your wonderment!

DAZZLING COCKTAILS

(Required: red cabbage, bicarbonate of soda and washing soda, three wine glasses with hollow stems, three paper parasols)

First of all, chop up some red cabbage and simmer it in two pints of water for ten minutes. Once this has cooled, strain the red water into a jug or clear bottle. Place the three wine glasses in a row on the table. Into the hollow stem of the first glass, place 1 teaspoon of bicarbonate of soda which has been dissolved in 100ml of warm water. In the second glass, place 1 tablespoon of washing soda which has been dissolved in 100ml of warm water.

Now you are ready to perform the trick! Give your audience three paper parasols, one blue, one green and one pink, and let them examine them thoroughly. Place the parasols in the glasses. Now take the cabbage water and pour some into each glass, and the colour will change immediately.

Make sure no-one drinks the cocktails. They may be a feast for the eyes but would not be at all pleasant on the tongue!

DINNER PARTY MAGIC

Replete with nourishment, you sit back contentedly and look for some entertaining diversion - preferably not too strenuous. What better diversion than some magic! These tricks cleverly utilise those objects found on dinner tables up and down the land.

DECEPTION IN THE BREAD BASKET

(Required: a bread roll and a coin)

You need to know how to "Palm" a coin in your right hand. Place it against the bottom joint of your middle two fingers and bend them slightly to keep the coin in place. Keep your other fingers curled and relaxed looking. Practice so that you can move your hand naturally but always keep the coin hidden from view.

To commence the trick, select a bread roll from the table and affect great interest in it. Examine it carefully and put your ear to it as if you can hear sounds from within!

Now hold the roll in both hands and press your thumbs down onto the middle so breaking the roll from underneath.

Press your fingers up into the roll from underneath, so pushing the coin inside. As you do this, break open the roll from the top thus revealing the coin in the centre of the roll. Practice this so that your movements are fluid and convincing. If you elect to practice in the privacy of your bedchamber, be prepared to sweep up the crumbs afterwards! Affect great surprise and delight as the coin falls from the roll but do not be surprised if your audience wish to experiment with their own bread rolls!

THE FAMOUS TUMBLING GRAPE

(Required: two grapes)

This is an utterly hilarious dinner party caper. You need to be within easy reach of some grapes and must still be sitting at the dinner table for this to work.

When the conversation is still animated and you are unobserved, you should secretly conceal a grape in your right hand by means of the Finger Palm. Hold it at the base of your second and third fingers, tense the muscles there so that grape is securely held in place. Make sure that your fingers are relaxed and slightly curled. You should be able to move your hand freely whilst keeping the grape hidden from view. Join in the conversation, wave your hand about freely, so no-one will detect the presence of the hidden grape.

When you wish to start the trick, announce that you can make a grape disappear and reappear in an unexpected place! Place another grape on the table, in full view of your audience. Pick up this grape using the thumb and fingers of your right hand and hold it so that the hidden grape is behind the visible one.

Put your hand to your mouth so that it looks as if you are placing the visible grape between your lips. In fact, you are placing the visible grape into your mouth and leaving the other one sticking out of your mouth but it must look as if you have only one grape in your mouth!

Now take the grape out of your mouth and hold it between the thumb and first finger of your right hand. Put your left hand over your right, as if to take the grape but actually let it drop into your right hand fingers. (This is known in Magic circles as the "French Drop" - see THE MELTING BALL SPOOF if you desire more detailed instructions.) Close your left fist and concentrate your gaze on it, pretending that it contains the grape.

It is most important that you remember NOT to attempt to speak at this point, or you will reveal the grape hidden in your mouth!

Drop your right hand casually and drop the concealed grape into a pocket. All the time you must misdirect attention to your left hand - raise it up, watching it intently. Suddenly flatten your left hand and hit the top of your head. At the same moment spit out the grape from your mouth and catch it in your right hand. This effect is a highly comical one and your startled audience should be delighted!

THE INVISIBLE ACCOMPLICE

(Required: a cocktail stick and a grape)

There is much scope for laughter in this trick, the more you can act the fool, the better! You need to be at a certain distance from your audience and, as you will see, the angle of observation is critical.

Firstly, point your first finger upwards and hide a cocktail stick behind it. Keep the tip of the stick hidden, just below the tip of your finger and keep it in place with your thumb.

To perform the trick, claim that you will attempt to balance a grape on the tip of your finger. Make it look as precarious as possible as you actually push the grape onto the stick but pretend to balance it on your fingertip. Always keep your palm towards you to hide the stick and concentrate very hard on the grape as you wobble your hand precariously.

This will test your acting ability to the full. It is possible to keep the company amused for a considerable length of time with your antics. You may wish to finish by eating the grape before challenging your spectators to have a go!

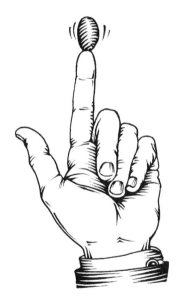

THE VANISHING CUP

(Required: a tumbler, elastic band and a handkerchief)

The best cup to use for this is a small plastic tumbler.

Before performing the trick, secretly place an elastic band around the top of a cup. It should fit snugly and be of the same colour so that it remains invisible.

Place a handkerchief on the tips of the fingers of your right hand and place the cup over your fingers. Use your left hand to stroke the sides of the cup as you talk, thereby slipping the elastic band off the cup and onto your fingers. Place the palm of your left hand on the base of the cup and turn everything over.

The cup will now be in your left hand while the handkerchief, because of the elastic band, remains covering the fingers of your right hand, which are still inside the cup. Hold the cup in your half closed left fist as it comes out from under the handkerchief. The elastic band will make it look as if you are still holding the cup with your right hand. You need to dispose of the cup in your left fist, perhaps by searching in your pocket for a magic wand. Once this is achieved, tap your right hand and pull away the handkerchief, flicking it towards your audience and call out "Catch!". When they perceive that there is no cup to catch, they will be amazed and astounded!

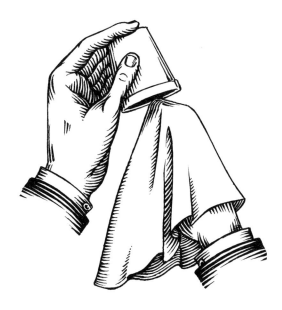

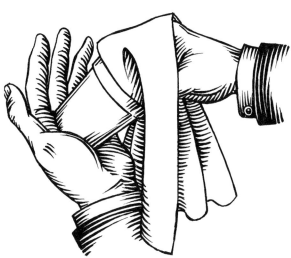

MIRROR IMAGE CAPER

(Required: two packs of playing cards)

For this you must appeal for an accomplice from amidst the congregation and give them one of the packs of cards. Desire them to shuffle their pack as you shuffle yours. Exchange packs and shuffle again. Secretly note and remember what the bottom card is as you shuffle. Exchange packs again.

Ask your accomplice to remove any card from his pack, look at it and memorise it. Say that you will do the same but in fact, do not attempt to memorise the card you pull out. Each selected card is placed on top of its pack and the pack cut once. So each card is now "lost" in its pack.

Exchange packs once again. Declare that each person is then to fan through his pack and remove the duplicate of the card they had originally selected. What you actually do is look for the card you saw previously at the bottom of the pack. Because of the way the packs have been cut, the card to the right of this one will be the card selected by your accomplice. As you each hold out a card, ask your accomplice if they believe in strange coincidences. You then both turn over your cards and they are seen to be IDENTICAL!

O the Powers That Be!

THOUGHT TRANSFERENCE

This is a most impressive mind-reading feat.

Ask your friend to think of a number between 1 - 9 (inclusive).

Ask them to multiply their chosen number by 9.

They should then add the two digits of the answer together.

Now request that they subtract 5.

Now beg them to imagine that each number corresponds to a letter of the alphabet: thus 1 = A, 2 = B, 3 = C and so forth. Ask them to think of a country which begins with the letter corresponding to their number.

Next, they should take the second letter of that country and think of an animal beginning with that letter. Lastly, could they think of a colour for that animal?

You are now master of the situation! Gaze intently at your volunteer and beg them to concentrate very hard. Finally declare, in a manner as deadpan as possible:

"Are you thinking of a grey elephant from Denmark?"

They will be utterly flabbergasted but in truth, the trick is very simple. Whatever number they originally thought of, the result of their calculation will always be 4. There are not many countries beginning with "D" so the rest follows suit.

If you do get some eccentric person who elects to choose an ostrich from the Dominican Republic - then you have been very unlucky indeed!

PUB MAGIC

All these tricks need is a handful of convivial persons assembled round a tavern table, several jugs of ale, some pockets full of change and the odd pack of salted peanuts.

A BAFFLING PRANK WITH A POCKETFUL OF CHANGE

(Required: six coins)

If the evening is passing slowly as you are supping with your friends in an alehouse, this is an extremely entertaining diversion. Suggest that everyone delves into their pockets and procure six large coins from the assembled company.

Place the coins in a circle on the table. Arrange them so that there is a random mixture of heads and tails uppermost. You may now invite your audience to participate. One by one, they are to come up and turn over TWO coins, one with each hand. Any number of spectators may do this and so it will turn out that some coins are turned over many times whereas others are not. All of this is to happen while you have your back turned or, if you are of a particularly dramatic kind, offer to leave the room until they have finished. Before you return they must cover ONE of the coins. This may be with a piece of paper or handkerchief, anything to ensure that the coin is completely obscured. After studying the coins for some

moments you will be able to predict whether the covered coin is heads or tails.

You achieve this remarkable feat thus:

As you turn your back, note how many tails are showing. You can easily predetermine this if you wish, as you are the person who arranges the coins in a circle. You only need to remember whether it is an odd or even number. When you turn to face the table again, note whether the number of tails now showing is odd or even. If it is the same as when you turned round then the covered coin is a head, if different, then it is tails. Remember "SAME - HEAD, DIFFERENT - TAIL"!

As you have a 50/50 chance of guessing correctly each time, you may need to repeat this trick several times in order to fully demonstrate your considerable power of insight. The fact that you predict correctly time and time again will produce rapt astonishment amongst the assembled.

A BIG DEAL

(Required: a pack of playing cards)

You need a fairly large company assembled to perform this trick, as you need to call for three volunteers. It is a particularly impressive feat of mind reading.

Firstly, take the pack of cards and remove the four Kings, the four tens and the two black twos as well as the Jokers. You must then deal the remaining cards, face downwards into seven piles. Ask three volunteers to each pick up one of the piles and to mentally select any card. Stress that they must not touch the card but that they must concentrate very hard on it and retain its image in their mind. Watch them carefully as they do this. Gather the piles up again. In order to ensure that your volunteers keep their image very clear, offer to give them a second look at the card.

Deal the cards again, but this time into six face down piles. Pick up one pile at a time and fan it out in front of each card chooser, asking them if their card is in that pile. If that pile does not contain a chosen card then discard it by placing the pile face up.

If a pile does contain a chosen card then close the pile up and close your eyes, declaring that you will now discover the identity of the chosen card. On all three occasions you will be completely correct!

The secret of your astounding powers lies in this subtle trick. You should think of the three volunteers as X, Y and Z and also, mentally number the heaps from one to seven, reading across from left to right. X will be the first to choose a heap and Y the second. Make a mental note of which heap each one chooses and turn the result into a three figure number. For example, if the first person chooses the fifth pile, the second the first pile and the third the fourth then you will have the number 514 in your mind. You must remember this number.

When you collect up the piles, do it so that pile 2 is placed on top of pile 1, and pile 3 placed on top of this etc. When you re-deal the cards into six heaps do not draw attention to the different number of piles.

If spectator Z, recognises their card in a pile you are holding up, you will know that it is the 4th card, counting from the bottom with the cards face upwards. In the same way, X's card will be the fifth card up and Y's card will be the first, or bottom card. You should note the identity of the card as you hold the cards up, then close up the pile and close your eyes.

The effect is best achieved if you are in no hurry to name the card, as it appears more impressive if you are striving to look into your volunteer's mind.

You should improvise along the lines of: "I would be much obliged if you would concentrate very hard on a mental image of your chosen card. Please concentrate firstly on the colour of that card....I am getting an impression of a black card. Is that correct? It is? Good. Now think very hard of the suit of that card...I am getting an image..it's a little unclear ...but I believe it to be a Spade. Correct? Excellent. Now for the most difficult part, please keep very still and concentrate on the value of that card. I need you to form a clearer image, please...Ah, it is becoming clearer to me now...Is your card the seven of Spades?"

This last, of course, is greeted with rapturous applause and amazement. You then proceed to do the same with each of the other two chosen cards.

You need to remove ten cards from the pack in order to have 42 (a number which is divisible by both six and seven). It does not matter WHICH cards are removed but it is a good idea to focus on the values rather than the number removed as the values are in fact irrelevant.

BOTTOMS-UP FOOLERY

(Required: three glasses)

This will encourage some lively audience participation.

Place the three glasses as shown in diagram (a). Tell your audience that you are able to put all 3 glasses bottoms-up in only three movements, turning two glasses upside down each time. You achieve it thus:-

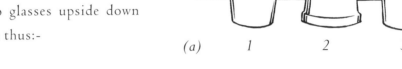

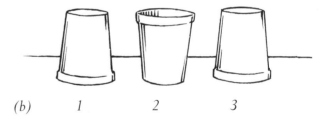

(a) 1 2 3

Turn glasses 2 & 3

Turn glasses 1 & 3

Turn glasses 2 & 3

Bravo! Now invite your kind audience to do the same but this time set your glasses up as in diagram (b). This is a trifle devious on your part but will not be noticed by your spectators. Even if your moves are followed exactly, they cannot accomplish the same feat. Do not be tempted to tease your patrons too much!

(b) 1 2 3

THE GREAT NUT RIDDLE

(Required: some nuts, an empty glass)

This demonstration of your mind-reading abilities will disturb and enthral your fellows. Place the empty glass and bag of nuts in the centre of the table. Inform your audience that they must follow your instructions exactly and concentrate very hard in order for the magic to work. Now turn your back and beg your companions to put a certain number of nuts in the glass, and the same number in a row on the table.

Next, they should take one nut from the glass, move it in a circle five times and add it to the row on the table. Then, ask them to recite the magic phrase "O-HO-CUS-PO-CUS", removing one nut from the table on every syllable and returning it to the bag. Beg the assembled to count the number of nuts remaining on the table and to take the same number of nuts from the glass and return these to the bag also. Finally they should remove a random number of nuts from the bag and replace these on the table. Ask them to cover the glass with a large handkerchief and you can then turn to face the table.

You will now endeavour to find out how many nuts are left in the glass even though you do not know how many nuts were in the glass to start with, or how many were removed. Concentrate hard on the row of nuts on the table before daring to pronounce "Is the answer three?"

Of course, you are exactly right! There will always be two less than the number removed from the table. As "O Hocus Pocus" has five syllables, the answer will be two less than five - three. You can repeat this trick and change the magic word just to thoroughly confuse your audience. Always remember that the answer will be two less than the number of syllables.

THE MYSTERY OF THE
UNDERCOVER COIN

(Required: a coin, glass of water, elastic band and a handkerchief)

For this you need a coin, a glass tumbler (half-full), an elastic band and a handkerchief or scarf.

Hold the glass in the palm of your left hand. Show your audience the coin and hold it, with the handkerchief draped over it, between the thumb and first finger of your right hand. Hold this over the glass, so that the handkerchief is draped over and concealing the glass.

Now allow the coin to drop so that the audience will think it has dropped into the glass. Secretly, you tip the glass backwards before you release the coin, so that it hits the side of the glass and actually falls into your left hand. Practice so that you can achieve this convincingly. Now straighten the glass so that it rests on top of the coin. The movement of the glass must be imperceptible.

Remove the handkerchief and the audience assume that the coin which they can see through the water, is lying INSIDE the glass.

Now replace the handkerchief and lift the glass up, through the cloth, with your right hand. Do not lift it so high that the coin will be revealed in

your left hand.

Concealing the coin in your left hand, put this hand in your pocket - ostensibly to get an elastic band. Use this opportunity to drop the coin into your pocket.

Place the elastic band around the mouth of the glass and place it on the table. Request that someone removes the band and handkerchief and retrieves the coin. Imagine their dismay when they see that the coin has disappeared!

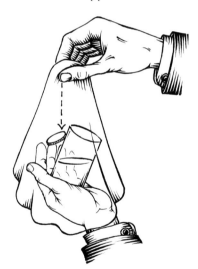

A NUMERICAL MIRACLE

(Required: pencil and paper)

A mysterious trick which requires no advance preparation or apparatus.

Ask one of the assembled to write down a three figure number on a piece of paper. Request that it be a fairly substantial number, a number, let us say, above 300. You proceed to do the same. Let us say that you write down 615.

Now take a third piece of paper. Gaze at your volunteer's forehead and scribble down something which you then fold up very small and give to him to keep.

Now reveal the number which you chose - 615 and beg him to add that number to his own.

"Is the result a four figure number? It is? Then please circle the last three digits. Is the circled number less than the number you originally wrote down? Yes? Then kindly subtract it from your number and write down the result."

Impress upon him that you have asked him to subtract a number which you do not know from another number which you do not know and yet, you can reveal the answer. In this instance, it is 385! Now ask him to look at the piece of paper which you gave him for safe keeping earlier. He will tremble to unfold the paper and find written on it, the number 385.

No matter what number your volunteer originally thought of, the final result will be 385. That is because the number you gave him to add to his own was 615 and

$385 + 615 = 1000$. In each case you must subtract your chosen number from 1000 to find the final answer. You can do this trick several times over, changing the numbers. For example, you could ask for a number over 600 to be chosen and chose 693. Simply subtract that from 1000 and the answer will be 307.

TURNING HEADS -
A BRAIN TEASER

(Required: ten coins)

Put ten coins in a circle, all with heads showing. Now set the following problem to your audience. The first coin touched is called "one", the next three must be touched and called "two, three and four". The fourth coin is then turned over so that it shows tails. The four taps can be made either clockwise or anti-clockwise, but they must all be made in the same direction.

The challenge is to continue doing this until only one head remains. The count must begin and finish on a head but the two middle coins can be either head or tails.

Your fellow revellers will puzzle over this seemingly impossible task for some time.

You achieve it thus: after turning over the fourth coin, always skip three coins before beginning the count again. Whether your first move is clockwise or anti-clockwise is unimportant, what is vital is that all subsequent moves MUST be made in the same direction.

If you carry the task out briskly, people will be unable to copy your moves. Be careful not to make it obvious that you are skipping three coins each time - perhaps let your finger wonder for a moment, as if you are unsure where to start the next count. Tease your audience. As ever, some devious acting on your part will add to the on lookers bafflement. You could invent an incantation, if you wish, and convince your audience that this lies at the heart of your miraculous ability!

CLOSE-UP MAGIC

These feats seem to invite the audience to crane forward for a closer view, yet the most kestrel-eyed amongst them will be none the wiser for all their proximity! These illusions will not render up their secrets even when performed in the most intimate of surroundings.

A KNOTTY PROBLEM

(Required: a length of rope)

No matter how close your audience get, they will never discover the secret of this trick. You can make a rope tie itself into knots - and they will never spot how!

Firstly, put the rope across both of your hands, with your palms facing upwards.

Raise your left hand slightly, turning it at the same time so that the palm faces towards you. Do the same with your right hand and a loop will form in the rope.

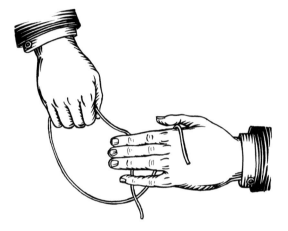

Next, place the loop over your left hand and over the end of the rope held by it. Lift the thumb to allow the rope to pass and then return it to its original position.

Repeat this two more times before putting down the rope. Pause to demand concentration and stillness from the audience. Build up an expectant atmosphere. Now, slowly lift up the end of the rope. As you do so, three knots will appear - as if by magic!

THE DANCE OF THE PAPERCLIPS

(Required: two paperclips and a strip of paper)

Using materials which are close at hand, this simple trick will delight and entertain even the youngest of infants.

Place the two paperclips on the paper, about an inch apart. Show this to your audience and claim that you can join the two paperclips together without removing them from the paper. Sounds impossible?

First of all, take the right hand side of the paper and tuck it under the left clip. Turn the paper over and do exactly the same thing again; tuck the right hand side of the paper under the left clip. Now take the two edges of the paper and pull sharply. The paperclips will fly up into the air - and they will be linked!

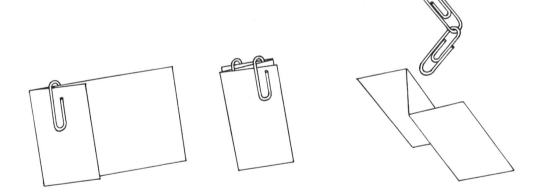

LISTEN CAREFULLY!

(Required: five small paper balls)

This highly entertaining trick will amuse all onlookers.

You need four small objects and one slightly larger - these could be coins, dice, sugar lumps or simply pieces of paper screwed up to form small balls. To prepare, secretly place one large ball in your pocket and hide one small ball in your right hand. In full view of the audience, place three balls in a row on the table.

Pick up one ball with your right hand and drop it into your left, counting out loud *"one"* as you do so. Do the same with another ball, count *"two"*, but at the same time, also drop the concealed ball into your left hand.

Pick up the third ball and pretend to drop it into your pocket, saying *"and one in the pocket"*. Actually keep the ball hidden in your hand, do not let go.

Pause, for greater effect, before opening your left hand and allowing three balls to drop onto the table - to gasps of astonishment, no doubt!

Pick up two of the three balls in your right fingers and drop them, together with the concealed ball, in your left hand. Again, say *"two in the hand.."*

and as you pick up the third ball and drop it in your pocket, say *"and one in the pocket"*. This time, really do drop it in your pocket but also secretly remove the larger ball. As your right hand comes out of your pocket, misdirect the audience's attention to your left hand which has opened to reveal that, once again, it contains three balls not the expected two!

Now pick up two balls from the table and pretend to drop them into your left hand as before, saying *"two in the hand"*. In fact, drop the large ball into your left hand and retain the two small balls in your right hand. As you say *"and one in the pocket"*, you pick up the third ball in your right hand and this time, drop all three balls into your pocket. It is a good idea to look at your audience as you do this; they will look at your face and not at your right hand.

Challenge your audience. Ask them to guess how many balls are in your left hand. Many will say *"2"*, others, more wary of having been caught out before, will say *"3"*. Now you can prove them all wrong by revealing the answer to be *"one"* and look, a single ball much increased in size!

ASTOUNDING CUP AND BALL MAGIC

(Required: three cups, four small balls and one larger ball)

This infamous trick is one all conjurors should master. You will need three cups which can be stacked on top of each other.

In preparation, place a large ball in your left pocket and one small ball in each of the three cups. Nest the cups, each one inside another, and conceal a fourth small ball in your left hand.

To commence your performance, place each of the cups upside down on the table. Do this smoothly and rapidly so that the balls stay in the cups as you turn them over.

Tap each cup and lift the first to reveal a ball underneath it. Lift the cup with your right hand and casually place it in your left, its mouth over the concealed ball as you direct all attention to the ball on the table. Repeat this with the second and third cups, revealing two more balls. As you pick up these cups, nest them on top of the one in your left hand.

[diag a]

Place the three cups, mouth downwards, one behind each of the balls. Place the first two cups to the right and left and the third cup in the centre. As you remove the last cup from your left hand, let the concealed ball drop into it. Unbeknownst to the audience, there is now a ball under the central cup.

[diag b]

Now pick up one of the balls and place it on top of the centre cup. Nest the other two cups on top. Tap the top cup and lift all three cups as one to reveal a ball on the table. It appears that the ball has passed through the base of the cup! Take time to acknowledge the applause that will undoubtedly occur at this point.

[diag c]

Again place all three cups on the table but place the middle cup (which contains the extra ball) in the central position over the ball on the table. Place a ball on top of this cup and repeat the previous trick. This time you will reveal two balls on the table when you lift the three cups as one.

Repeat the trick, but this time allow a spectator to tap the top cup. This diversion allows you to take the large ball from your pocket and hold it in your left hand. Lift all three cups as one to reveal three balls on the table and casually place the cups over the large ball in your left hand.

[diag d]

Place all three cups on the table as if the trick were now finished. Appear to hesitate before declaring "Ladies and Gentlemen, against all the rules of Magic I will now venture to reveal a secret unto you. I do indeed use more than three balls to perform this feat". Your beholders will be dumbfounded to see the large ball under the cups.

ASTOUNDING CUP AND BALL MAGIC

(continued)

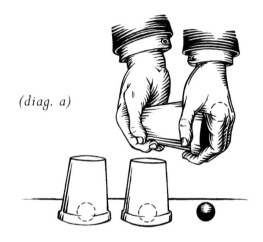

(diag. a)

(diag. b)

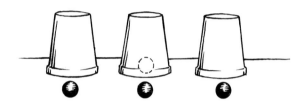

(diag.c)

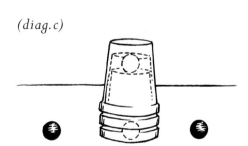

(diag. d)

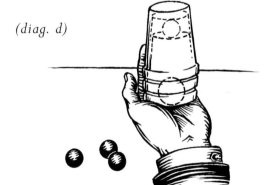

MIGRANT MONEY MYSTERY

(Required: five coins)

Place four coins on the table as in the diagram. You need to have a fifth coin concealed in your right hand. You will probably find that the easiest way to hold this is between the thumb and first finger, at the base of the thumb. Explain to the assembled that you are only allowed to cover two coins at any one time. Cover coin 1 with your left hand and coin 4 with your right hand. Then change position so that the right hand covers 2 and the left hand covers 3. Secretly pick up the coin at 3 and drop the concealed coin at 2. Raise your hands. There are now two coins at 2 and none at 3. One coin has "travelled" from one corner to another.

Move quickly on. Move your left hand, with its concealed coin up to 2 as your right hand goes down to 4. Drop the concealed coin at 2 and pick up the coin at 4. Raise both hands to show that another invisible journey has indeed been made!

Now, as your audience are left reeling, cover 1 with your left hand and 2 with the right. Secretly lift up the coin at 1 and drop the concealed coin at 2. Raise both hands and bring them together at the edge of the table. All four coins will now be at 2. You need only drop the concealed coin into your lap and accept the applause.

1   *2*

3   *4*

CONFOUNDING COLOURS

(Required: a pack of playing cards)

This should be the "piece de resistance" of your act. It depends on your ability to pre-arrange the pack and to master a False Shuffle. This enables you to seemingly thoroughly shuffle a pack and yet ensure that certain cards, or indeed the whole pack remain unaltered in their position.

These shuffles must be practised regularly and Remember! Do Not Look at Your Hands While You Perform a False Shuffle!

Hold the pack in your right hand, in the normal position for shuffling. Drop about half of the cards from the top of the pack into your left hand. Then drop all of the remaining cards on top. Pick up the whole pack from your left hand and repeat these moves as often and as fast as you can. All you are doing is cutting the pack repeatedly but with practice, it will look as if you are shuffling the pack thoroughly. This keeps the whole pack in the same order.

Now for the trick:

Secretly arrange a pack so that the first two cards are red, the next one black, then red, then two blacks then one red, followed by 23 blacks and 22 reds. You need to be able to remember the sequence of the top seven cards. Give the pack a False Shuffle so that the entire pack remains in order.

Claim that you can indeed sense the colour of a card without looking at its face. Take the first card and predict that it is red. Turn it over. Continue naming the colours of the first seven cards before turning them over and place the two colours into two separate piles as you deal them.

After you have dealt the first seven cards, claim that this wisdom lies within your audience also. Ask a spectator to deal the remaining cards into two vertical rows beneath the cards you have already dealt. Entreat him to separate the cards according to colour without looking at the faces. Secretly count the number he deals and when he has dealt 23, ask him kindly to stop.

Declare that you are about to complicate things a little further. Remove one of the face-up cards from the red pile and place it face up at the bottom of the "black" pile and place one of the face up black cards at the bottom of the "red" pile. Your spectator should now continue dealing, but this time place the cards of each colour he thinks right beneath the new marker cards.

When dealing is complete, ask your spectator to turn over the cards in the left column. The cards beneath the black marker are all black and those beneath the red marker are all red!

The other column is now incorrect but you have an opportunity to correct this while the other column is being revealed. Scoop up the cards and spread them face up from left to right until the first marker card is revealed (which will be face down). Spread the rest of the cards in a line above the ones you have just put down. The marker cards are actually in the wrong place but if you can leave them face down, the effect of this trick is so startling, it is unlikely anyone will notice. Once again, flagrant misdirection and flamboyance will cover all.

RED ALERT

(Required: two packs of playing cards)

Another trick which tests your powers of mind-reading, this is fascinating and will intrigue all on-lookers.

You need to have two sets of playing cards with differently coloured backs, let us say, one blue and one red.

Take eight playing cards with blue backs, one red card with a blue back and one black card with a red back.

Arrange the cards so that they look like the following illustration ie; alternate face up and face down cards, all black faces and blue backs showing.

Announce that you are about to make a prediction and write on a piece of paper "You will choose the red card". Request that one of the attendance safeguard this paper but do not reveal its contents.

In order to choose a card, ask one of your spectators to choose any number from 1 to 10.

If they choose 1,2,5,6,9 or 10, SPELL the number from left to right, tapping one card for each letter as you do so.

If 3 or 4 are chosen, COUNT along the line from left to right.

If 7 or 8 are selected, COUNT along the line from right to left.

In this way, whatever number is chosen you will end up on either the third or fourth card from the left.

Now reveal your prediction. If it is the third card, turn all the others face up to reveal that they are all black. If it is the fourth card, turn it over to reveal that it is indeed red. Either way, your prediction is proved CORRECT!

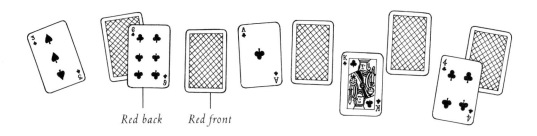

Red back　　*Red front*

ROLL UP, ROLL UP

(Required: a pack of cigarette papers)

This is an amusing diversion which requires a modicum of advance preparation. Take out one of the cigarette papers, screw it up into a tiny ball and hide this under the top paper on the pack.

To perform the trick, remove the top paper taking the rolled-up paper still hidden in place behind it. Use your thumb to keep the rolled-up paper concealed. You should be able to show the audience both sides of the paper as your thumb completely covers the rolled-up ball.

Now tear the paper into half and half again. Keep tearing until you have a series of small pieces which you can squeeze into a ball. Use this "squeezing" motion to bring the concealed ball into view and hide the torn pieces between your thumb and finger. In effect, the two pieces of paper "change place".

Utter a magic incantation over the paper and slowly unfold the ball to reveal that the pieces have "re-formed". Now you will be holding a piece of paper with a small ball concealed behind it. Allow a moment for your spectators to fully take in this astonishing feat, then crumple up the paper, wrapping it around the torn pieces. and dispose of it.

A fun variation on this is to give one of your fellows their own set of papers, and instruct them to copy your actions as you do them. Much laughter will ensue as their pieces fall to the floor and you reveal your restored paper. The resulting hilarity will also afford you ample opportunity to pocket the torn pieces.

THE TRAVELLING COINS

(Required: six coins and a ring)

This is an astonishing trick which is guaranteed to impress even the most cynical of observers. You must practice it thoroughly until you are fully conversant with the sequence of moves and your movements are dexterous and nimble!

Arrange the six coins in two rows of three and place a small ring to the right of this. This ring could be borrowed from one of your audience. To commence the trick, pick up the ring and three right hand coins in your right hand. Be sure to hold the coins so that they are held in the crotch of your thumb. Pick up the other three coins in your left hand and say *"Three coins in my left hand"* and slap them down on the table again.

Pick up the coins again but this time hold them so that they are at the bottom of the fist, alongside the little finger. Place the left fist on the table top about 4 inches from your right hand and say *" And three coins and a ring in my right hand"* as you apparently drop the coins and ring on to the table. What you

actually do is release only the ring from the right hand. At the very same instance, you move the left fist to the left, leaving its three coins on the table as your right hand comes down on top of them. When you raise your right hand, three coins and a ring can be seen. These appear to have come from your right hand but of course you still have three coins in this hand, unbeknownst to the audience. This is not a difficult move but it does need practice as the whole trick depends on the success of this movement.

Now, pick up the three coins and ring with your right hand. This must be done naturally so that the coins already hidden there are not revealed. Place your right hand under the table.

Slap your left hand on the table and then lift it to reveal that the coins have gone. Remove your right hand from under the table and roll all six coins plus the ring onto the table. The coins in the left hand appear to have passed straight through the table.

You audience will be amazed.

THE WONDERS OF NATURE!

(Required: two large and two small balls, a handkerchief)

First you need to learn the secret of one of the classic magical manipulations: the Thumb Palm.

This is the means by which you hide small balls in the palm of your hand. Press a ball into your palm and close your thumb slightly so that the ball is held in place and gripped by the muscle at the base of your thumb. The ball should feel quite secure between your thumb and first finger. If you curl your fingers slightly and keep them relaxed, no-one will know that you have a ball hidden in your hand.

Now for the trick:

Secretly palm two small balls in your hand. In view of your audience, place two large balls on the table. Ask the assembled to examine them thoroughly and then cover them with a handkerchief. As you lay the cloth over the balls, release the two hidden balls and leave them underneath the cloth. You should practice this until you are confident that no-one can see the moment of release.

Wave your magic wand over the cloth or say a magic word before lifting the handkerchief to reveal two balls have grown into four!

TRAVEL TRICKS

These tricks are good for travellers and what better way to break the ice when you find yourself sharing a carriage with a stranger. A simple deck of cards will divert you and your fellows from your attendant discomforts and transform your journey into a delight.

A GATHERING OF ACES

(Required: a pack of playing cards)

This trick may seem rather difficult at first but it is worth persevering with. Go through the moves very slowly until you have mastered it - your time and trouble will not have been wasted as your compatriots will remember this trick as one of the most enjoyable they have ever seen.

To start the trick, go through the pack and remove the four Aces, placing them face upwards on the table.

Hold the pack face downwards in your left hand, away from the Aces, and ask one of your patrons which their favourite Ace is. It is important to be direct and hold their gaze as you speak to them. Your spectators will now be looking either at you or at the Aces spread on the table. This gives you the opportunity to accomplish the following move: spread the top three cards slightly to the right and insert your little finger under the third card. You have just made a "break" which you mask by squaring up the pack with your other hand. Your audience should be unaware of what you have done.

Let us suppose that your patron's favourite ace is the Ace of Clubs. Pick up this card and place it face-up on the pack. Place the other Aces, also face upwards, on top of this.

Lift off the top seven cards (those above the break caused by your little finger.)

Use your left thumb to pull the top Ace to the left. Call its name out and use the remaining cards in the right hand to flip the Ace face downwards unto the pack.

Repeat this with the next two Aces. You will now have the Ace of Clubs in your right hand with three face down cards hidden under it.

Now drop ALL these cards, but handling them as if they were ONE, from your right on top of the pack in your left. Turn the Ace of Clubs face down as you say "lastly, your favourite Ace, the Ace of Clubs". Thus your patrons believe there to be four Aces on top of the pack,

whilst in fact, there are now three different cards between the Ace of Clubs and the other Aces.

Deal the first four cards face-down onto the table, in a line. Put three cards down on top of each of these, making sure that the first three cards (the Aces) go on top of the Ace of Clubs.

Beseech one of your patrons to choose a pile. Allow him to think that he has a free choice but in fact force him to pick the pile with the Aces in it, by means of Forcing The Choice.

You may Force The Choice by a process of Elimination. In this instance there are four piles, a,b,c, and d and you wish to force (a). Beg your patron to choose two piles. If they touch b & c or b & d or c & d then simply remove them. If they touch (a) and another pile the regard these as having been chosen and remove the other two. Either way, you are now left with your desired pile (a) and another. Ask for one pile to be pushed towards you. If (a) is pushed, remove the other pile as if a had been chosen. If the other pile is pushed simply take it away, leaving (a). Thus pile (a) will appear to have been freely selected.

Pick up each of the discarded piles and reveal the cards. The assembled believe there to be an Ace at the bottom of each pile but you show them that these Aces have Fled!

Now turn dramatically to the "chosen" pile and reveal these cards one by one. The Four Aces have gathered themselves together!

DISASTER AVERTED

(Required: a pack of playing cards)

In this illusion you will cause a chosen card to transmogrify itself - to disintegrate and reintegrate in a different position in the pack. Pass the cards from a shuffled pack, one by one, before your spectators' eyes, counting them as you do so. He is to note a card and remember both it and its position in the pack. Do this very slowly and carefully so that a choice will be made before you reach, say, fifteen. Then stop and replace the fifteen cards on the pack in the same order.

Direct your attention to another of the captive and ask them to choose a number between fifteen and thirty. (The upper limit of thirty is merely so that the effect is not dragged out for too long). Now, entreat both of your volunteers to concentrate on their chosen numbers. Place your hands behind your back as you gaze intently at each of them in turn. Beg their assistance as you attempt to look into their minds.

What you are actually doing behind your back is to divide the pack in halves and place them face to face. Turn the pack so that the original top cards become the lower half and bring the pack forward. Hold the cards ready to deal and remind your audience, the card and numbers have been merely THOUGHT of, you have asked no questions so you can only find out by Reading Their Minds.

"What was your number, Sir?" you ask. "Eight? I thought so. Let me show you that your card has left that position" You deal out seven cards and turn over the eighth. He agrees that this is not the card he had chosen.

Now turn to your second volunteer: "What number did you think of, Madam?" "Twenty? Just as I thought. Let us see if the card has arrived at that position."

Now you must subtract the first number from the second number (in this instance 20-8=12). This is the number of cards you can turn over before you have to reverse the deck. You have already dealt 8 cards, so 4 remain. Continue dealing cards face down onto the table, counting 9,10...When you reach the twelfth card, pause before you place it down. "Ladies and gentlemen," you declare, "Twelve is my lucky number, and I am tempted to take a chance here. Is this card, in fact, your card?"

Throw the card face upward on the table, and at the very same time, drop your left hand a little and turn it so that the back of the hand is uppermost. In effect, you have now turned the pack over.

"Not your card?", you exclaim in disbelief! Appear momentarily bewildered, pause, reconsider, then recommence. "In that case Madam, I believe my original purpose has been achieved" Continue the count very deliberately, the cards now coming from the original top of the deck.

When you reach the number twenty, place this card face down apart from the others. Solemnly declare unto your audience that the card selected was selected Mentally, that you have asked for no clues at all. Ask for the card to be named and then turn it over.

This has the most brilliant and startling effect. The turn of the pack is made at a point where when the audience have no cause for suspicion and the final cards are dealt openly and fairly. Always remember to subtract the first number from the second and turn the pack at this point. Calling this your "Lucky Number" is a blatant piece of Misdirection.

ODDS ON FAVOURITE

(Required: a pack of playing cards)

An illusion which requires that some cards be pre-arranged, this set up is virtually imperceptible. This time a 9, 7, 5, 3 and Ace are placed on top of the pack each one with a different card between them and three indifferent cards on top of these.

A spectator chooses a card and is requested to write its name down on a piece of paper, fold this and put it in his pocket. Whilst he is doing this you make a break under the ace. Cut at this point and let the spectator replace his card there. False shuffle the pack.

(See "CONFOUNDING COLOURS" for details of how to perform a False Shuffle)

Proceed to hand the shuffled pack to the spectator and entreat him to deal the cards from the top, slowly, stopping at any card as the spirit moves him. Tell him that by noting the number of spots on the card, and continuing to deal that number of cards he will find his chosen card.

What you must do is, tell him he can stop only after he has dealt three cards (so that he cannot stop at one of these). Ensure that the deal is made very slowly so that he will stop before the Ace is reached. You must keep track of the alternate cards as he deals them, (the 7,5,3 and Ace). If he stops with one of these in his hand tell him to turn it over, but if he stops with an indifferent card in his hand, tell him to turn over the top card. The number of spots on this card will tell him how many more cards to deal before he finds his card.

When you spread the cards for the spectator to choose one, you must run the cards off very quickly, in threes say, until you reach the twelfth. Make sure that this point is reached before he has a choice to draw a card and then spread the rest so that a "free" choice can be made. You can, if you like, make the little finger break at this point. Be sure to hold the pack well down in your hand as the cut is made so it is not seen to be near the top, have the card replaced and you can then square the deck openly and in full view. It is also vital that the deal is made very slowly.

A DOUBLE BLUFF

(Required: a pack of playing cards)

Countless card tricks depend on a spectator taking a card and the Magician identifying this card. There is a special manoeuvre which will enable you to move a returned card to the top of the deck though it appears to be lost in the middle. It is a move often referred to as "making the pass".

The card is returned to the top of pile (a). Pile (b) is then placed on pile (a) so that the cards form a "jog" - one pile projects over the other. Keep the fingers open a little to allow space for the cards to slip forward a little and hide the jog. Turn the cards on their side. Lift pile (a) out and place it on the other side of pile (b). It looks like the chosen card is in the middle of the pack but you can now reveal it to be on the top. PRACTICE until this is effortless. This is the basis of the following trick:

Ask a member of the audience to choose a card and then return it to the pack. Using the above method, move this card to the top of the pack.

Request your subject to tell you the name of his chosen card. Lets say it was the Queen Of Clubs. Now spell out the card's name as you deal out the cards face down, say "Q" as you lay down the first card, "U" for the second and so forth until you come to the final card, the "S" of clubs. Turn this up with a flourish and then feign great concern and dismay - O Horror! It is not the right card! Drop this final card on top of the face down heap, castigating yourself gravely. Now pick up the heap you have dealt out (at the bottom of which, you know but the audience does not, is the Queen Of Clubs.)

Steal yourself for your final essay. Ask your subject to be so kind as to help and spell out each letter as he deals each card himself. You may at this point introduce any hokus pokus word or incantation you wish for of course this time, the last card he deals proves to be The One!

A DOUBLE BLUFF

(continued)

(a)

(b)

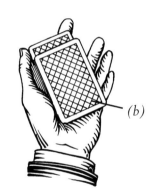

(b)

(a)

(b)

(a)

THE ROVING COIN

(Required: a coin and a piece of paper)

Place the coin on a piece of paper. Fold the bottom edge up to within half an inch of the top and then fold back both sides. Finally, fold the top back. The coin appears to be securely enclosed within a package, but in fact, the top edge is open. Turn the package over in your hand so that this open edge is at the bottom. Tap the coin with a pencil or, preferably, a magic wand, to show that it is still there. Now allow the coin to slip out of the packet into your hand. Keep it secured in your palm.

Now you may tear up the packet with a dramatic flourish. Lo! The coin has disappeared.

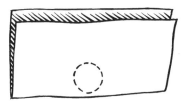

A VERITABLE MYSTERY OF
THREES AND FOURS

(Required: a pack of playing cards)

In order to perform this trick you need to be able to shuffle a pack and retain the top batch of cards in their position.

To do this, begin to shuffle but on the first drop of cards, make sure that you take at least 8 cards onto your left hand. Shuffle the rest of the cards on top but slightly to one side. When you have finished shuffling, there should be a definite "step" in the pack. Cut the pack at this point and place the cards from the bottom, (in this instance the original 8 cards) on to the top.

It looks as if the cards were fairly shuffled and then cut but in fact the top cards will be in exactly the same order. Practice until you can accomplish this easily.

To perform this illusion you must prepare the pack beforehand by putting the four fours on top of the pack and on top of these, the four threes. In full view of your audience, give the pack a false shuffle, retaining the order of the top 8 cards. Deal the first eight cards out in a row, face down and ask a member of your audience to pick a card and push it forward (still face down). Pick up the remaining cards from left to right, tucking each card picked up below the previous one.

Start dealing the cards out into a pile and when you have dealt at least seven cards ask a spectator to cry "stop" whenever they wish.

Stop dealing at this point and put the remaining cards to one side.

Gather together the cards already dealt and hold them in your left hand. Declare that you will now deal the cards into a number of piles according to the value of the card selected. (ie. either 3 or 4).

If you deal the cards into 3 piles, turn over the top card of each pile and Lo And Behold you will uncover three threes.

If four piles, then four threes will be revealed.

This is an impressive trick and, no matter, how hawk-eyed your friends are, they will never discover its secret!

CHILDREN'S PARTY TRICKS

These tricks are easy for juveniles to perform and appreciate; they present an ideal starting point for the budding magician. Fancy sleights of hand are kept to a minimum so that instead, the dear child can concentrate on developing their own individual style of presentation and flair.

THE ABSCONDING RING

(Required: rope, a ring and a handkerchief)

Knot the ring on a length of rope as shown in the diagram. Knot the ends of the rope together so that the ring is trapped and ask one of your audience to hold the knotted ends whilst you keep hold of the ring. Use a handkerchief or piece of cloth to hide the ring from sight.

Tell your audience that you will now endeavour to free the trapped ring - without untying the rope. Urge your accomplice to hold onto the rope with all their might!

With your hands underneath the cloth, free the ring by loosing the knot (as in fig c) and pushing the rope downwards over the ring. As you do this, utter the magical word "Vamoose!", very firmly. Lo! - the ring is now free, yet the rope remains knotted!

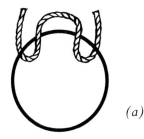

(a)

(b)

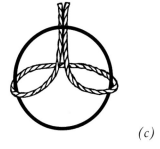

(c)

THE ENCHANTED DICE

(Required: one dice, a pencil or wand, cardboard tunnel)

Firstly, you need to make a Magic Tunnel as shown below. You will need to use light card, and the tunnel should be a little larger than the dice you intend to use. Half way along one side you should cut a hole large enough to tip the dice as it is pushed along the tunnel (see diagram c).

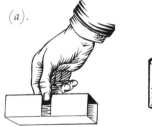

(a).

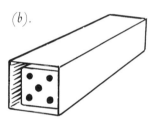

(b).

To commence the trick, hold the flattened cardboard tube in your hand and show it to your audience. Tell them that when a dice is passed through this tunnel, the number on the dice will magically change! Then fold the cardboard into its tunnel shape. It is most important that you keep the hole out of view at all times, keep it on the bottom side and cover it with your thumb so no light shows through. Practice this, as your handling of the tube will determine whether or not the tick works. Now take a dice and place it in the passageway with, let us say, the number 1 forward. Show the audience that this number is foremost. Turn the tube sideways to the audience and using a pencil, (or preferably a magic wand), carefully push the dice through the corridor. As the dice hits the hole in the centre it will topple over and a different number will be showing on the dice as it reaches the end. Whatever number is on top of the dice as you place it in the tube will end up facing forward. You can repeat this trick to your dumbfounded audience as often as you like, as long as you are careful to always keep the hole in the tube concealed.

(c).

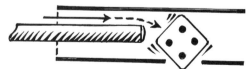

THE EXTRAORDINARY
LEAPING DICE

(Required: four dice, a cardboard tunnel)

For this trick you need to possess a "Magic Tunnel". (See page 84 "THE ENCHANTED DICE" for details of how to make one.)

It is important that one of the four dice is of a different colour. Let us say, for sake of example, you have three red and one blue dice. A little advance preparation is called for as you secretly place one of the red dice at the bottom of the tube. It is important that the audience do not know that it is there. So you should hold the tube so that the pressure from your hand keeps the dice in place and prevents it from being seen.

To start the trick, put the tube on the table. It is very important that you keep the hole towards you (ie. hidden from view). Pick up the blue dice and put it in the tube. Place the two red dice on top. Your audience will believe that the order of dice inside the tube is blue, red, red. Now lift the tube, holding it at the top and actually lifting the top dice with the tube. When the tower of dice is revealed, it is shown to be red, blue, red: it looks as if the blue dice has "jumped up" one place. Your audience will be perplexed that the red dice is no longer at the bottom of the pile!

You can bewilder you audience further by continuing the trick. Turn the tube over and put it down on the table so that the hidden dice is now at the bottom again. This time, put the blue dice in second. Again, it will have appeared to have "leapt" up a floor. Always be careful to lift the tube so that the top dice comes with it. Keep this hidden and your secret will never be revealed!

THE MUTATING ROPE

(Required: two pieces of rope, one long and one short)

A little advance preparation is called for here. First, tie a short piece of rope around the centre of a long piece. The two ropes must be of the same colour. Do not tie it too tightly. Now tie the two ends of the long piece of rope together. It should look like you have two equally long pieces of rope, tied together.

To perform the trick, show the ropes to your audience and tell them that you can make these two short pieces of rope into one long piece.

Untie the real knotted ends and pretend to examine the rope. "Mm, that leaves a knot in the middle of the rope" you can exclaim, "maybe I should try using a magic word!". Ask your audience to suggest all the Magic Words they know while you wind the rope around your left hand. Keep winding as you come to the false knot, but actually hide the knot as you slide it along the rope and into your right hand. Keep that bit of rope hidden in your hand as you mutter your chosen magic word.

Your audience will be lost in wonder as you let the rope unwind from your left hand and reveal that it is now one piece.

PROFESSOR OF PRESENTIMENT

(Required: three pieces of card, large and small envelopes, paper)

This mind reading trick requires some advance preparation but is well worth the effort!

On the first piece of card, draw a red spot. On the back write "This is the colour you will choose"

On the second card put a green spot and on the last a yellow spot. On the back of both of these write "You will not choose this card"

Take the paper and write on it, "You will choose the green card". Put this in the smaller envelope and seal it. On the front of the envelope write "You will choose the yellow card". Place the small envelope in the larger one and seal it also.

To perform this trick you should ask a volunteer to choose one of the cards. Be careful not to reveal the backs of the cards as you display them to your audience.

Encourage your volunteer to change their mind as often as they wish, make sure they are completely happy with their choice. Ask them to reveal their choice to you and respond confidently "I knew that would be your choice"

Your method of revealing their choice depends on the colour chosen:

If RED is chosen, simply turn over the cards one at a time, ending with the red one.

If YELLOW is chosen, open up the envelope and take out the smaller one, revealing the message written on it.

If GREEN is chosen, take out the smaller envelope with the message side towards you so the audience cannot see it. Take out the slip of paper and show it to the audience.

This illusion is completely foolproof!

A WITTY POSTCARD RUSE

(Required: a postcard, scissors)

Tell your gentle friends that your special powers enable you to pass your head right through a postcard!

Take a postcard and fold it in half lengthways. Make a series of cuts along the length of the card from the outside edge towards the folded edge. You must not cut right through to the fold.

Now turn the card so that the folded edge is towards you and make a series of cuts IN BETWEEN the other cuts, cutting from the fold towards the edge, but not right up to the edge.

Finally, unfold the card and fold it again, this time width ways. Make a cut along the centre fold - again not right to the edge.

Now the card is ready! Carefully open it up and you will find that you have a hole big enough to pass your head through.

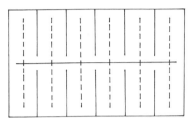

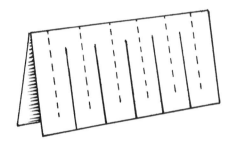

RISQUE MAGIC

These tricks are greatly enhanced by being performed in mixed company. They encourage some gentle fraternisation between the sexes, so naturally should only be practised amongst those whose minds are pure in intent.

THE IMPRISONED MAIDEN

(Required: two long pieces of rope)

Address your audience "I would be much obliged for two intrepid volunteers - a gentleman and a lady". Tie one piece of rope around the wrists of your obliging gentlewoman. Firmly fasten the ends so that the loops cannot be slipped over her delicate wrists. Do the same with the second rope but slip the free end around the already fastened rope before tying it. Thus your lady and gentleman are effectively "handcuffed" together!

Challenge them to free themselves without unfastening the ends or cutting the rope. Their efforts will be highly amusing - but in vain! To spare your victims blushes you can eventually declare that you will attempt the task.

You separate the two thus: Draw the middle of one of the ropes towards the opposite person, forming a loop as marked in the diagram. Draw the loop towards a wrist of the opposite person. Pass the loop through the string around the wrist, in the direction wrist to hand and then pull it over the hand.

Now draw the rope again round the wrist but in the opposite direction, hand to wrist. The two cords will become free and the couple separated.

With practice, you will be able to achieve this at great speed.

This trick is most effective if you can conceal your movements. You could cover the ropes with a scarf but then you must practise so that you can manipulate the ropes without being able to see them. Alternatively you could position your body so that your actions are concealed, occasionally looking over your shoulder at the audience in mock confusion. Once you know how it works, you could also try this trick with yourself as one of the "prisoners".

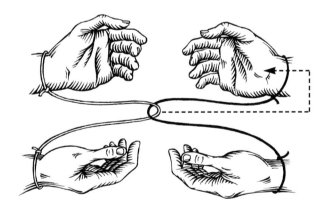

POWERS OF PERSUASION

(Required: a plain postcard, pencil and playing cards)

You need a sizeable gathering of maidens and youths in order to perform this mind-reading trick, as you will need to call on three different volunteers.

Firstly, you need to learn the subtle art of 'forcing' a card, whereby an innocent spectator unwittingly chooses the very card that you want them to take. Here is the easiest method of achieving this. If you want the King of Diamonds to be chosen, make sure that this is the card on the bottom of the deck. Place the pack on the table and ask a spectator to cut the pack in two and then place the bottom half cross wise on top of what was the top half. You should then proceed with the rest of this trick so that the audience will forget what exactly has happened. When you come back to the cards at the end of the trick, ask your volunteer to take off the upper portion of the pack and look at the card they have selected. This card, the bottom card of the top portion, is in fact the card which was at the bottom of the deck, the King of Diamonds. Once you have mastered this, it is time to learn the complete trick.

To perform the illusion, Write the numbers 1,2, and 3 on the postcard and show it to the audience.

Request that the first volunteer cut the pack as requested and then explain that you will return to the cards later. Now ask your volunteer to think of the name of someone whom they secretly admire. Gaze into their eyes and say that you will write down the name of

that person. In fact, write down King of Diamonds under the number 3. Do not let your audience see this. Ask them to divulge who they were thinking of. When they tell you, look at your card and appear pleased or indeed, relieved.

Now turn to a second spectator and ask them to think of a particular characteristic of their loved one of which they are particularly fond. Again, gaze at them and then write down the name of the person previously selected under number 1. Ask what the characteristic is and look thoughtfully at your card.

Now ask a third volunteer to look at the "selected" card (see above). Ask them to think very clearly of that card as you write down the name of the characteristic under 2 on your postcard.

Ask a further volunteer to take your card and read out your predictions.

Correct on every count? It will appear more realistic if you have got one of the predictions slightly wrong (maybe you selected "teeth" as an admirable quality for example!) But two out of three predictions will surely impress. This is but the bare bones of a trick which you can really embellish and have fun with. You can invent other categories and try and get your audience to be as revealing as you dare. In every case though, you will correctly predict the card chosen.

TWO'S COMPANY

(Required: two long pieces of rope, two rings and a wand)

The "magic wand" could be something as humble as a pencil, knitting needle or ruler.

Hang the two ropes over the wand and tie both sets of ends together in a basic knot. Pull the knot against the wand but do keep it quite loose. Ask for a lady and a gentleman to kindly come forward from the audience and ask each to hold a pair of rope ends. Before they take their rope ends, pass each pair of rope ends through one of the rings.

Now ask each volunteer to hand you only one of the two ends they are holding. Tie these together in a single knot and hand the ends back to your volunteers. Again, secure the knot but do not hold it too tight. The arrangement should resemble that in the diagram and the rings appear to be securely knotted - now for the flourish!

Impress on your volunteers the gravity of their responsibility. They must not disport themselves immodestly or let go of their rope ends. Hold both rings and the ropes in your right hand. Carefully slide the wand out, keeping hold of the rings in your right hand. Keep hold of the knots and pull the rings down firmly with your left hand. The rings will come free even though the spectators are still holding the ends of the ropes, and the knots will disappear.

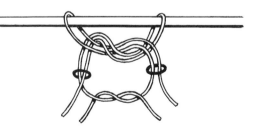

A BREATHTAKING COIN RELEASE

(Required: a coin and a silk handkerchief)

The handkerchief should be purloined from a lady present. As she sees her dainty silken scrap apparently destroyed, her screams of dismay will doubtless prove a useful distraction!

Hold the coin between the thumb and first finger of your left hand and drape the handkerchief over the coin. Grasp the coin, through the material, with your right thumb and forefinger. Lift the coin a little and then replace it in the left fingers.

Unbeknownst to your audience, this movement enables you to make a slight adjustment in the silk. As you replace the coin in your left fingers, you obtain an extra fold of material between the coin and your left thumb. (diag a)

Now, lift the front edge of the handkerchief and drop it over the other side of your left hand.(b)

Next, move your left hand forwards and over, so that the thumb is facing down. This is a very simple movement yet its effect is quite brilliant. The coin will now be outside and to the back of the handkerchief.(c)

Turn the left hand slightly and use your right hand to twist the material under the coin so that its shape can be seen through the cloth. The top edge of the handkerchief is folded over the coin so that you can hold it in place securely and the coin seems trapped within the cloth.

Hold the twisted cloth with your left hand to stop it unfurling. Use your other hand to gradually pull the coin up and out of the handkerchief(d). You should make it look as if the coin is actually penetrating the lady's silk. Once the coin is out, you need to open the handkerchief quickly before the frightened damsel reaches for her smelling salts. Show that the coin's journey has left no hole in the cloth!

A BREATHTAKING COIN RELEASE

(continued)

(a)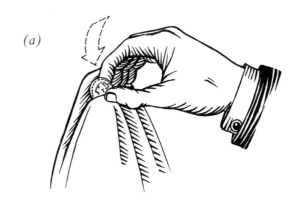

(b)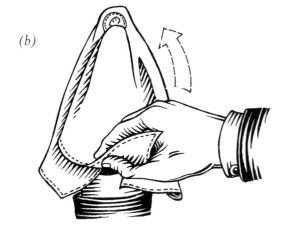

(c)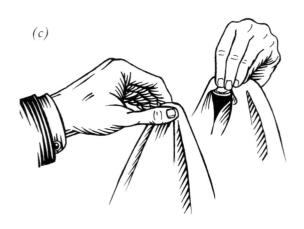

(d)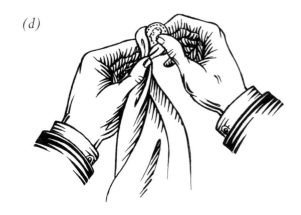

THE WICKED
QUEEN OF THE NIGHT

(Required: a pack of playing cards)

This trick centres on that notorious lady of the night, the Queen of Spades, a personage skilled in witchcraft. Let the pack be thoroughly shuffled by one of the company, then run through the cards face upwards in order to remove the Queen of Spades. Place this card face down on the table, to spare the ladies blushes.

Explain that you require only three dozen cards so ask a volunteer to cut off about a third of the pack and place this to one side. The remaining cards should be dealt into three piles. You must then turn your back on the action, whilst your volunteer chooses one of the heaps and shows the top card to the assembled company. The other two heaps should be then discarded.

When you turn to face the table, you will see one pile only. Point out that there is no way you can know either which heap was chosen or which card selected. Neither can the Queen of Spades know for she has been lying face down all this time. Ask your volunteer to kindly shuffle the chosen pile and lay the cards face up in a circle. As you reach for the Queen of Spades, appear to hesitate and be so bold as to suggest a further complication: it may be a good thing to have the cards face down so that the Queen cannot see their faces.

Take up the Queen of Spades and slowly pass her over each card in the circle. Affect tremblings of the hand as she reaches one of the cards. "She is receiving signs" you whisper. Beg your volunteer to reveal the identity of the selected card. "The Four of Spades (say)?". The Queen's choice is turned over and is revealed to be the very card, The Four of Spades.

The effect is achieved thus: When you look through the face-up cards to pick out the Queen of Spades, note the three cards facing you and memorise them (ie. the three cards which will be at the bottom of the pack when it is face down). Only one of these cards will be in the face-up circle and it will be the chosen card. A subtle finger movement by you will assist the Queen's excitement as it reaches this card.